LISA SLATER

A-Z OF BLOGGING

Fisher King Publishing Ltd,
The Studio,
Arthington Lane,
Pool in Wharfedale,
LS21 1JZ,
England.

www.fisherkingpublishing.co.uk

A CIP catalogue record of this book is available from the British Library

Print ISBN 978-1-910406-71-7

Contents

About the author

Lisa Slater started out as a professional freelance copywriter in 2014 after gaining diplomas in both Feature Writing and Copywriting.

In 2017, she launched Make Your Copy Count Ltd and created two training workshops; Blogging for Business and Write to Sell.

Prior to starting a career in copywriting, Lisa worked overseas for nine years and travelled extensively, before settling in Leeds with her husband in 2012.

Lisa is passionate about writing and hopes that the 'A-Z of Blogging' will inspire others to share their thoughts, ideas and knowledge using the written word.

Introduction

Thank you for purchasing the 'A-Z of Blogging'. The aim of this book is to give you the skills and confidence to create an engaging business blog that gets results.

What is a blog?
The word 'blog' derives from the word weblog. Blogs originally started out like online diaries where people wrote about their day and shared thoughts and ideas.

People soon realised that blogs could be used as a marketing tool for businesses. In some cases, blogs are a business in themselves, generating revenue through advertising.

These days, blogs can be about everything and anything; people share observations, ideas, news, advice, information and knowledge.

The key difference between a blog and a standard website is that a blog is updated regularly with new content. Many blogs are now integrated into business websites and used to attract more visitors to the site.

In this book, we refer to blogs in terms of written online content for marketing purposes. However, much of the advice can be applied to hobby blogs, video, printed articles and other forms of content marketing.

How to use this book
You can read this book from cover to cover or dip in and out as you need. Each chapter covers a standalone subject related to blogging, but many of the topics are closely linked.

If you are just starting out in blogging, then you might find it beneficial to start with 'D is for Direction' where you'll learn about strategy. You can learn about the more technical side of backlinks, keywords and optimisation once you've got to grips with the basics.

Alternatively, you may prefer to just dive right in, starting with 'A is for Analytics' where you'll learn more about measuring the success of your blog against your objectives.

At the end of each chapter, you'll find a 'bonus tip', a list of related chapters and a summary of the key points. These 'chapter takeaways' can be used as a refresher as you build your blog.

Every effort has been made to keep the book jargon-free. If there are any terms you aren't familiar with then use the handy glossary at the back.

Approach this book in whatever way works best for you. The tips and advice can be applied straight away or built in as your confidence in blogging grows.

About Make Your Copy Count Ltd
Make Your Copy Count is a copywriting agency in West Yorkshire, providing high-quality copywriting services to SMEs.

As well as writing copy, they also edit and proofread all types of documents, and provide excellent training around blogging and copywriting.

You can find out more about Make Your Copy Count at www.makeyourcopycount.com

Analytics

Measure your results

A is for Analytics

Most businesses start a blog because they want to get results. The main objective could be to increase social media engagement, drive more traffic to your site or raise brand awareness.

Establishing the purpose of your blog helps you build a strategy, but how do you know if you're achieving your goal?

When you set sales targets, you keep track of whether they are being met. Marketing is just the same; you need to measure the outcomes to ensure what you're doing works.

Monitoring and understanding your analytics allows you to identify what type of blog content your audience engages with most and which posts aren't generating as much interest. This will help you focus your blog content to ensure that you attract your target audience.

Google Analytics

Google Analytics is essential if your goal is to increase website traffic. As well as being able to check if the number of visitors is increasing, there are other useful metrics too.

You can see exactly where your visitors are coming from so you can focus your marketing efforts more effectively. You'll also get insights into the behaviour of visitors; which posts attract the most readers, how long do they spend on your site and are they taking the desired action?

Google Analytics can be confusing at first but fortunately, there are loads of great online guides that can help you get to grips with the ins and outs of it all.

The Google Analytics course for beginners from Google covers all the basics in an easy to understand video format.

Social Media Analytics

If you blog, then you probably share your blog posts on social media. The great thing about social media is you can see at a glance if people are engaging with your posts through the number of likes, shares, follows and comments.

If you really want to understand exactly who is engaging and whether your call to action is working, then check your analytics.

The use of social media as a marketing tool for businesses has increased substantially so most platforms now offer plenty of insights into your audience and their behaviour. Twitter, Facebook, LinkedIn, Instagram, YouTube and Pinterest all allow you to view engagement and activity for each individual post.

Use analytics to measure results

Whatever you want to achieve from your blog, you need to measure the results. If you don't measure, then you won't know what works. Understanding your analytics helps you make more informed decisions about the content you share and how you share it.

A is for Analytics: chapter takeaways

- Decide what your objectives are and how you will measure these

- Set up Google Analytics for your website or blog at www.google.com/analytics

- Track the relevant metrics

- Learn how to read your social media analytics

- Use your analytics to concentrate your marketing efforts more effectively and create more of the blog posts your target audience want

Related chapters

D is for Direction

M is for Marketing

S is for Sharing

T is for Target audience

Backlinks

Build good inbound links

B is for Backlinks

Backlinks are links from one web page to another. Occasionally you see a URL written in full, for example, https://www.makeyourcopycount.com, but usually, the link is included as a clickable link using relevant anchor text.

Quality backlinks are great for improving search engine optimisation (SEO) because they show the search engines that your blog or website has content that people want to share. Backlinks also help search engines crawl your site and index pages faster.

Not all backlinks are good

Firstly, backlinks should be relevant. You wouldn't want someone linking to your blog about growing tomatoes using the anchor text 'learn how to get rich quickly'. When the reader clicks the link, they will see the content doesn't match and they'll click straight off your site.

Paying for links is also a bad idea and can land you in trouble with Google. Avoid inbound links from spam sites, porn sites and automated sites and don't spam forums with links to your blog where it isn't relevant to the topic.

Don't just post links to your blog on the comments sections of other people's articles. If your blog post genuinely relates to another article, then privately contact the author and ask if they would mind including a link to your post.

Google will penalise sites that try and manipulate page

rankings through dodgy link schemes. Focus on building natural, high-quality links.

How to get good inbound links

The good news is that there are ways you can earn quality inbound links.

Creating quality content that people want to share is the most natural way of getting inbound links. Blog posts that are informative, interesting or entertaining will earn more links organically. The more effectively you market your blog, the more people there are who are likely to see it and link back to it.

Guest blogging is also an effective way of building links, but there are some things to watch out for with this. Don't write guest posts that are purely for linking purposes; if you are guest blogging for someone else then make sure your posts are of value to their target audience.

There is nothing wrong with contacting related businesses and asking them if they would be happy to share your content or allow you to create a guest post for them. Do make sure that you only approach reputable companies that you want to be associated with. Refer to chapter 'G is for Guest blogs' later in this book for more advice on guest blogging.

Outbound links

As well as getting quality links to your site, you need to ensure that you are only linking to reputable sites yourself. Avoid links to spam sites or companies that you do not know or trust. You may be penalised for linking to poor quality websites.

> **Bonus Tip**
>
> *As well as linking to external sites, make sure you include plenty of internal links within your blog. Link to other blog posts, product pages or services that relate to your post. This makes it easier for search engines to crawl your site and for readers to navigate around it.*

B is for Backlinks: chapter takeaways

- ➡ Quality backlinks help improve SEO

- ➡ Not all backlinks are good

- ➡ Don't spam comments sections or forums with links to your blog

- ➡ Creating high-quality content is the best way to earn quality inbound links organically

- ➡ Guest blogging can help build links to your site

Related chapters

G is for Guest blogs

O is for Optimisation

U is for Uniqueness

Z is for Zzzz

Call to action

Ask the reader to take action

C is for Call to action

A call to action (CTA) is a direction to the reader telling them what to do next. In online sales, marketing and advertising it is usually an instruction such as 'buy now', 'order today', 'subscribe', 'donate', 'sign up', 'join now', 'register', 'click here', 'add to basket' and so on. An online call to action is often in the form of a button or hyperlink.

Why does a blog need a call to action?

Business blogs are usually used as a form of marketing to attract the attention of your target audience, build a relationship and eventually turn them into a customer or client. Having a call to action helps keep readers engaged for longer and moves them to the next stage of the process.

Your CTA might differ depending on where you have acquired the reader and whether they are a new or returning visitor to your blog, a potential customer, repeat customer or ongoing customer.

The purpose of your call to action could be to:

- Ask readers to follow your business on social media

- Subscribe readers to your blog

- Link to a product or services page

- Direct readers to related blog posts

- Encourage comments on your blog by posting a question

- Persuade readers to download a document/

catalogue/brochure

- Get readers to make an enquiry or contact you

- Request readers' email addresses in return for something free

Make sure that your call to action relates to your blog post so that it is a logical next step for your reader. You can use more than one CTA in a post to lead readers towards different actions. For example, you could have a 'subscribe to our blog' sign-up as well as social media share buttons and a 'contact us' button.

Creating a stronger call to action

Top tips to make your call to action stronger:

- Use strong verbs; "**buy** now", "**order** today"

- Offer something free; "download a **free** copy of our latest e-book"

- Use emotion; "book a holiday your family will **love**"

- Keep it simple

- Make your CTA stand out by using bold, coloured or large font or creating a clickable button

Measure results

The purpose of a call to action is to get a reader to take that action. To check how effective your call to action is, you should measure your results.

You can use Google Analytics to see exactly how many visitors you are getting to your blog post. You can then compare how many of those readers are taking the required action and work out how successful your call to action is.

C is for Call to action: chapter takeaways

- A call to action moves the reader to the next stage

- Keeping readers on your blog or website for longer is good for SEO

- Keep your call to action simple

- You can include multiple calls to action on your post

- Make call to actions clear

Related chapters

A is for Analytics

D is for Direction

L is for Layout

T is for Target audience

Direction

Make sure you have a blog strategy

D is for Direction

Without a defined blog strategy or clear direction for your blog, it is very hard to know if your blog is effective. After all, if you don't make it clear what results you want, how do you know if you are achieving them?

Defining exactly what the purpose of your blog is, what outcomes you expect and how you will achieve them, means you are more likely to get the result you want.

If there is more than one contributor to your blog then the blog strategy will act as a guide to ensure everyone is working toward the same goal. It also helps simplify decision making such as choosing subjects for your blog posts.

What your blog strategy should include

If you want results from your blog then take time to put together a strategy. The first thing you need to decide is what you want to achieve:

- Increase online presence
- Attract larger social media following
- Build brand awareness
- Establish yourself as an expert
- Generate leads/enquiries/sales
- Get more website traffic
- Improve SEO

When you've established what you want to achieve, you

can build your strategy around this. Things you need to consider are:

- Who is your target audience?
- How will you market your blog?
- How will you generate ideas for your blog?
- Which format will you use?
- How often will you blog?
- How will you measure your results?

Implementing your blog strategy

Once you have a clear direction for your blog then you need to stick to it. Write down your strategy. It doesn't have to be a fancy document, as long as you answer the above questions. Refer to this document every time you are generating ideas or writing your posts. This will help you keep your blog on track. Measure your results to ensure that your strategy is working.

> *Bonus Tip*
>
> *Your blog strategy should be aligned with your overall business strategy. What is your company mission and vision? How will your blog strategy fit with this?*

D is for Direction: chapter takeaways

- ➡ Answer the following questions:

    - ○ What are your desired outcomes?

    - ○ Who is your target audience?

    - ○ How will you market your blog?

    - ○ How will you generate ideas for your blog?

    - ○ Which format will you use?

    - ○ How often will you blog?

    - ○ How will you measure your results?

- ➡ Refer to your blog strategy regularly to make sure you stay on track

Related chapters

F is for Format

M is for Marketing

Q is for Quantity

T is for Target audience

Editing

Perfect your post at the editing stage

E is for Editing

Editing your blog post is the most important stage. Nobody sees your first draft so it doesn't matter if it is badly written. The editing stage is where you perfect your post and make it the best it can be.

Don't try and write and edit your post at the same time. If you leave a break before editing, you'll go back to it with fresh eyes. It's easier to spot mistakes and be more objective.

Write your post and leave it overnight before going back to edit. If you can leave it a week then that's even better.

Top tips for editing your blog

Deliver on the headline
Does your blog cover what the headline suggests? Have you covered the subject sufficiently?

If you promise a solution to a problem make sure you give a solution. Don't specify ten tips and only give nine. Read your post through the eyes of your target audience; would your post meet their expectations?

Cut out waffle, word repetition and jargon
When you write, it can be easy to repeat yourself as your ideas flow onto the page. The editing stage is where you cut the waffle and remove any repetition. Avoid repeating words at the start of a sentence or using the same adjective multiple times.

Be wary of industry jargon; use reader-friendly terminology. If you are using acronyms, write them out in full the first time you use them.

Eliminate words and phrases that don't add anything
If you can remove a word without it changing the meaning of the sentence, then ~~just~~ delete it. ~~Very~~ often, we include words that don't ~~really~~ add anything. Eliminating them makes your copy stronger.

Words such as "really", "very" and "quite" can be easily cut as shown in the above paragraph. Words like these are sometimes referred to as 'weasel words'. Weasel words add nothing to a sentence and should be removed.

See Appendix 1 for a list of common 'weasel words'

Ensure consistency
Make sure you are consistent throughout your post with capital letters, hyphens and the way you write dates. If you have referred to 24th September 2017 in the first paragraph, don't later write 24/09/17. If you have capitalised every word in the first sub-heading, make sure you format all the subheadings in the same way.

It can be a good idea to create a 'style guide' that you can refer to every time you write and edit a post. This helps you keep consistency across your website and blog. A style guide can be a simple text document listing how you will write certain words, what words you will capitalise and how you will format information such as times and dates. It can be added to as your blog develops.

Present your point logically
When editing, you may need to reorder paragraphs so that your points are presented in a logical order. Don't jump from one idea to another and then back to the first

idea as it is confusing for readers.

Make your headline and intro strong

Headlines are a crucial part of your blog post and you should take time to get them right. Refer to the chapter 'H is for Headlines' later in this book for more detail on creating a strong title.

Once your headline is strong enough to draw readers in, don't lose them with a weak intro. When you get to the editing stage, pay particular interest to your first paragraph and make it as engaging as possible.

Summarise and include a call to action

Don't let your blog post fizzle out. Summarising the key points is an effective way of ending a blog post. Include a call to action; invite readers to comment, ask readers to share your post or subscribe to your blog or direct them to related articles.

Proofread

Proofreading is a vital stage of the process; you don't want your blog to be let down by spelling mistakes or stray apostrophes.

You will pick up some errors as you edit but we recommend leaving your blog again after editing and then giving it a final check before publishing.

Don't rush the process, write, edit, then proofread. This ensures a higher quality blog post.

E is for Editing: chapter takeaways

- ➡ Write first and edit later. Cut unnecessary words and phrases

- ➡ Ensure consistency throughout your post

- ➡ Make sure your post presents information logically

- ➡ Pay special attention to the headline and introduction

Related chapters

C is for Call to action

H is for Headlines

P is for Proofreading

W is for Writing

Format

Decide which post formats are right for
your blog

F is for Format

Blogs come in different formats depending on the subject, objective and target audience. Here are some popular types of blog:

Which format is best for you?

Different blog formats work better for different types of business and you need to decide which is right for you. Consider your target audience, subject and blog strategy when choosing your format.

You may choose to stick to one format for all your blog posts, or you may prefer to switch between a few different types of blog. These are some of the formats that work particularly well for business blogs:

List posts

List posts are the most popular type of blog post. They provide useful information and are easy to scan, which makes them more appealing to readers.

List posts have a higher click-through-rate than other types of post, especially when a number is included in the headline. Examples of list posts include:

- Top 10 tips for...

- 101 best/worst...

- The 15 best... for beginners

- The 5 most popular...

- 50 money-saving tips for...

- 37 ideas for...

- The 25 most inspirational...

- 7 reasons why...

- 25 websites that...

Instructional

How-to posts and tutorials provide readers with valuable information and give businesses a chance to demonstrate expertise in their field. These kinds of posts work well as video, text or a combination of both. Step-by-step guides and checklists also make great instructional posts.

Informational

Industry news, tips and techniques, research findings and explainer posts are all types of informational blog. Many people search the web for information; if you can provide that information, you establish yourself as an expert whilst building awareness of your brand.

Predictions and reviews

These make great posts at the start or end of a year. Write a review of the major changes in your industry over the last 12 months or give your predictions for any developments in the year ahead.

If there has been a change in legislation or a new development, then write your forecast of how it will impact the industry or review the changes.

Case studies

Case studies are useful for giving readers an insight into your company but you should alternate them with other types of blogs too. A company blog that only has case studies will not keep readers coming back.

When writing a case study, give the reader an outline of why the client needed your help then detail what you did and what the outcome was. It is good practice to include a quote from the client verifying that the outcome met or exceeded their expectations.

News posts
Industry news, company news, local, regional or world news can all make great subjects for blog posts. Explain the latest developments, let readers know how it will impact them or give your opinion on a subject. Refer to the chapter 'N is for News' later in this book for more advice on using news in your blog.

Interviews and profiles
Interviews or people profiles can make interesting blog posts. You can write about people in your company to give readers an insight into your brand, or interview industry experts to give your readers an alternative view on a subject.

Categorise your posts

If you are using different formats or writing on different subjects then categorise your blogs so that readers can easily find similar posts.

For example, you could have 'case studies, product reviews and interviews' as categories, or 'industry news, top tips and how-to guides'. When a reader selects a category, they can view all posts that match that format.

Alternatively, include links to similar posts at the bottom of each blog post.

F is for Format: chapter takeaways

- Decide which formats work best for your business
- You don't have to stick to one format
- List posts are the most popular type of post
- Choose the most appropriate format for the subject
- Categorise your blog posts to make it easier for readers to find similar posts

Related chapters

H is for Headlines

J is for Journalism

N is for News

U is for Uniqueness

Guest blogs

Guest blogging provides many benefits

G is for Guest blogs

Guest blogs are blog posts written by an outside source. It could be an industry expert, a specialist in your area or someone that offers complementary services to yours. For example, a web designer may ask a copywriter to provide a post on top tips for writing homepage copy. This is useful content for the web designer's target audience and helps the copywriter promote their services.

A guest blog can be you creating a post for somebody else's blog or inviting somebody else to write a post for your site.

Guest blogs are attributed to the person writing them and usually include a link back to the author's own site. This is not the same as ghost-writing, content writing or copywriting, where someone is paid to create content that will be attributed to somebody else or their company.

Benefits of guest blogging for another business

More exposure
Your blog will be seen by readers and subscribers of the company blog you are writing for. The company will also be sharing your post on their social media pages which will raise your online profile and attract more followers for your business.

Establishes your credibility
If you are invited to guest blog for another company it shows you are considered an expert by that company. This helps you build credibility and brand awareness.

Creates inbound links

Your guest blog will include a link back to your website. Quality backlinks are good for search engine optimisation and will also increase your traffic, especially if the blog you are writing for has a high readership.

Benefits of inviting someone to guest blog for you

Attract new visitors

If someone writes a post for you, then chances are they will share that post on their social media pages which will bring new visitors to your site.

Provides a different viewpoint

By asking somebody else to write about a subject, you give your readers a new viewpoint. This helps keep your content fresh and interesting.

Associate your company with other experts

If the company guest blogging for you has a good reputation in their industry, this helps you build credibility. It shows your readers and their readers that they are happy to be associated with your company.

Tips for guest blogging

Whether you are guest blogging for someone else or inviting someone to write for your blog, there are a few things to remember.

Be selective

Guest blogging for the sake of guest blogging is pointless. Not only is it a waste of your time, but it can also be detrimental. Linking to or from spam sites or non-reputable companies is bad for SEO and your reputation.

Make sure you choose companies that relate to your industry, products or services or who share a similar target audience. If you sell gardening equipment then writing for a beauty blog isn't beneficial. Their readers are coming to their blog to read about beauty, not gardening, so your content won't engage them. Even if you do write a beauty related post, linking it back to your services will be pretty difficult.

Establish topic/length/style/format of post
If you are writing a post for someone else, ask if they have specific requirements for the topic, format or word count. It is also important to understand who their target audience is to make sure your content is relevant.

When asking someone else to guest blog for you, inform them of any specific requirements you have. Make sure you set the expectations.

Agree on a deadline
If you are asked to guest blog, find out when you need to send the finished article and ensure you meet this deadline. If the company has a publishing schedule and you don't deliver on time, then you could damage your relationship with them.

Ask for guest posts to be sent at least a week before you plan on publishing them. This gives you a chance to check you are happy with the content and ask for any amendments to be made.

Share
One of the benefits of guest blogging is that it increases the online presence of both the company hosting the blog and the company writing the post. Once the post

has been published, make sure you share it so that you reach more readers. Ensure the other company is also sharing the post so that you both benefit.

Guest blog for companies you trust

Guest blogging is an excellent way of getting exposure but make sure you only associate your business with businesses you trust. If you are approached about guest blogging, take time to research the company before you agree. Don't guest blog for companies you don't feel comfortable with and don't post anything on your blog you aren't happy with.

> ### Bonus Tip
>
> *Establish in advance whether images are needed and who will provide them. Make sure you have permission to use any images used so that you don't infringe copyright. Refer to the chapter 'I is for Images' for further information on this.*

G is for Guest blogs: chapter takeaways

- Guest blogs are attributed to the person who has written them

- Guest blogs help increase exposure and build brand awareness

- Make sure that you share the guest blog to ensure maximum exposure

- Agree any specific terms or requirements in advance

- Work with companies that you are happy to be associated with

Related chapters

B is for Backlinks

I is for Images

M is for Marketing

S is for Sharing

Headlines

Create attention-grabbing titles

H is for Headlines

Blog headlines are often hailed as the most important part of any blog post. After all, if nobody is clicking on your post in the first place, then nobody is reading it. If nobody reads your blog, then all the hard work you put into researching, writing and editing goes to waste.

Consider how many headlines people are exposed to online every day as they scroll through news feeds and social media. If your headline doesn't grab their attention, your post goes unread.

Statistics show that on average, only 8 out of 10 people read a headline and only 2 of those people will go on to read your post. A powerful headline will increase that number so you get more clicks, more readers and more shares.

Top tips for creating blog headlines

Be clear
Make it clear to the reader what your post is about. What will the reader get from reading your post? What's in it for them? If the reader cannot work out from your headline what the post will be about then they probably won't read it. The reader wants to know what to expect.

Be honest
Don't be tempted to lure readers in by using misleading headlines that don't match up to your content.
There's no point grabbing a reader's attention with clickbait headlines only to lose them straight away when they realise your post doesn't deliver what you promised with the title.

Be concise
Headlines that are too long will get cut off in search engine results so it's important to keep headlines as concise as possible. Cut out unnecessary words to make your headlines stronger.

Instead of: "These top 10 tips for writing blog headlines will help you get more readers"

Try: "10 tips for creating click-worthy headlines".

Optimise
Your headline should include a keyword or phrase. This helps more readers find your post, improves SEO and makes it clearer what your post is about. Try to include your keyword at the start of your title when possible. Using a colon can make this easier.

For example, if your keyword is "blog titles" then;

Instead of: "The ultimate guide to writing blog titles"

Try: "Blog titles: the ultimate guide"

Headlines that work

There have been many studies into what makes a headline more effective. Researchers have looked at everything from how many words a headline should contain, to which words and phrases get the best response. Here are some proven ways to create stronger headlines:

Use numbers
Various studies have shown that using numbers in headlines improves the click-through-rate.

Examples include:

- 10 tips for...

- 7 ways you can improve your....

- Increase your sales by 350% using...

- Only 27% of businesses...

- 101 ideas for...

- What would you do with an extra £250 a week?

- The average business wastes over £5000 per year on...

Offer solutions
Blog posts that offer a solution to a problem are extremely popular. How-to posts, top tips, checklists and step-by-step posts all work well. Give advice that makes something easier, quicker, simpler, faster or helps improve, reduce, fix or increase something.

Use negatives
Research shows that negative headlines have a higher click-through-rate than positive ones. Headlines containing words such as; "worst", "avoid", mistakes" and "never" get a better response. Sometimes it can be better to write a post from a negative point of view rather than a positive.

Instead of: "10 tips for a better blog"

Try: "Avoid these 10 blogging mistakes".

Use interesting adjectives and inspire emotion
Power words like "free", "limited", "rare" and "bargain"

appeal to our greed or fear of missing out. Words such as "love", "delighted" and "amazing" invoke positive emotions. "Recommended", "official" or "tested" are words that inspire trust.

Use interesting adjectives in your headlines such as "epic", "ultimate" or "awesome" to get more attention.

See Appendix 4 for more great examples of power words

Ask a question

Headlines that ask a question appeal to readers because they automatically get the reader thinking about the answer.

"What will... mean for you?

"Could you be missing out on...?"

"How does... affect your business?"

"Are you wasting money on... ?"

"Are you struggling with... ?"

"Would you like to know the secret to...?"

Measure your success

Test different types of headline and use your analytics to see which types of headline are the most successful. This will help you create stronger headlines going forward.

H is for Headlines: chapter takeaways

- An attention-grabbing headline will earn you more readers
- Make sure your headline matches the blog content
- Headlines with numbers in get more clicks
- Negative headlines attract more readers
- Use power words in your headline

Related chapters

E is for Editing

F is for Format

J is for Journalism

W is for Writing

{ Ii }
is for

Images

Don't get caught out by copyright issues

I is for Images

Using images in your blog posts makes them more visually appealing. On social media feeds, posts with images attract more attention than those without. If your blog post is long, then images break up the text.

When using images, you should include an alt tag. This gives people who are using screen readers a clear description of what the image is. It can also be optimised by including relevant keywords. Refer to the chapter 'O is for Optimisation' for more information on alt-tags.

Copyright

When you use images for your blog or website, you must ensure that you do not infringe copyright. Copyright infringement can lead to legal action and even criminal prosecution.

Photographs, images and illustrations are automatically protected by copyright. Unless the creator gives permission for their image to be used, you are not permitted to share, copy or distribute that image.

Usable images

Using images for your blog may sound like a minefield but the good news is there are plenty of images you can use without fear of copyright infringement.

Public Domain
Public Domain images are free for use. These include images where the copyright has expired or the creator has waived their rights. You can use these images for personal or commercial use. The only exception is where

the image includes a recognisable person as you may need permission from the model as well.

Creative Commons licences
Creative Commons licenses allow creators of images to waive some or all of their copyright rights. There are six different CC licences. Images with a CC 2.0 licence mean you can use the image if you give attribution.
A CC0 licence means the creator has relinquished all copyright rights to the image.

Royalty free
This means that you pay a fee for the image and are then allowed to use it without giving attribution or paying additional royalties and fees.

Attributing images

When attributing images, you should include the title, details of the author, the original source and details of the license. You should also include details of any modifications you have made to the original image.

Sourcing free images

Fortunately, there are hundreds of websites offering public domain, CC0 and royalty free images for you to download and use for free.

Pixabay
Pixabay offers royalty free and CC0 licensed photographs, illustrations and graphics for you to use for free.

Unsplash
Unsplash offers a large collection of high-res images all available for free under their Unsplash licence.

Pexels
Pexels images are available under the CC0 licence so you can download and use for free without attribution.

Public Domain Archive
Public Domain archive offers a range of images available for free download.

Stokpic
Stokpic was set up by a sole photographer and now hosts a vast collection of beautiful free images available under the Stokpic licence.

Canva
Canva is a great tool for designing unique graphics. You can create infographics, social media banners, blog headers and document templates as well as many other graphics. Canva is fun and easy to use.

Check the terms

It is your responsibility to ensure that you use images in line with the permissions that have been granted. If you use a site offering free stock images, check their T&Cs or licences before sharing any images that are not your own.

I is for Images: chapter takeaways

- Using an image in your blog post is recommended

- Include alt tags when using images

- Make sure you don't infringe copyright; ensure you have the correct permission or attribute correctly

- Use public domain images, royalty free images or images with a CC0 licence

- If using stock images, make sure you check the T&Cs of the website you are downloading from

Related chapters

K is for Keywords

L is for Layout

O is for Optimisation

V is for Video

{ **Jj** }
is for

Journalism

Use journalistic techniques

J is for Journalism

You don't need formal qualifications or training to become a blogger but that doesn't mean that you don't need certain skills to be successful.

Just like a journalist writing for a newspaper or magazine, you must present information in a way that is interesting to your reader. Master the following key journalistic skills to improve the quality of your blog.

Generate ideas
A journalist must be able to source news stories and ideas for features; similarly, you need to generate ideas for your blog posts.

There are many types of blog format to choose from. Sometimes the format of your blog may dictate the subject, whilst other times the subject will determine the format. Refer to the chapter, 'F is for Format' earlier in this book for more in-depth information on types of blog post.

See Appendix 3 for tips on generating ideas

Conduct research
You need to do research to ensure the information used for your blog is accurate, especially if the subject is not one you are completely familiar with. If you are blogging about a widely covered topic then you can set your blog post apart by going into more detail and offering more facts. This requires a little more effort at the research stage but will give your readers a better experience. Refer to the chapter, 'R is for Research' later in this book for more in-depth information on research techniques.

Interview effectively

You may not always need to interview for your blog post but, if you do, then it's worth taking some time to learn effective interviewing techniques. This ensures you get the most out of your interview so you can create a better blog post.

Tips for effective interviewing:

- Pick the right location; avoid noise and distraction

- Think about what you want to gain from the interview in advance

- Plan your questions before the interview

- Let the interviewee know what the purpose of the interview is so they feel at ease

- Keep the interview natural and make the interviewee feel comfortable

- Record information accurately; if you struggle taking notes, bring a second person or use a recording device (with permission)

- Don't be afraid to ask for more detail or rephrase questions if you don't get a sufficient answer

- Ask open questions and get personal insight

- Present quotes correctly; misquoting an interviewee can result in libel action if the person believes it is damaging to them or the reputation of their company.

Report accurately

Providing incorrect information, misleading statements or false claims can be very damaging. At the very least, you look dishonest or uninformed. In the worst cases, you will incur legal action against you or your company. Depending on your industry, you may be breaching compliance regulations. Don't cut corners when it comes to researching and fact-checking.

Act within the law

Journalists must act ethically and adhere to media and journalism law. As a blogger, this is also important. You must act within the law when it comes to basic privacy rights, discrimination, copyright law, defamation, the disclosure of personal information, data protection and misuse of information.

Your blog is a representation of your company or organisation so keep it professional.

Write, edit and proofread

Whether you are writing for a newspaper, magazine or blog, you need to write clearly, edit effectively and proofread carefully. Having a good command of the language you are using is important. You should at least learn the basics of grammar and punctuation if you want to write quality blog posts. We recommend you leave gaps between writing, editing and proofreading.

Create attention-grabbing headlines

Journalists use headlines to grab the attention of the audience. Whether the story or feature is for newspapers, magazines, radio or TV, the headline is important. Writing a strong headline for your blog post is equally important.

When you share your post, you want to attract readers; a well-written headline helps you do that. Refer to the chapter, 'H is for Headlines' earlier in this book for more tips on titles.

J is for Journalism: chapter takeaways

- Good bloggers require similar skills to journalists

- Accurate research is important

- Learn effective interview techniques for better interview based blogs

- Act within the law and be morally and ethically responsible when writing your blog posts

- Pay attention to headlines

Related *chapters*

F is for Format

H is for Headlines

R is for Research

W is for Writing

Keywords

Include keywords naturally

K is for Keywords

In search engine optimisation (SEO), keywords are words or phrases that provide an overview of the content of a web page. They help search engines match your web page to the search term that someone has entered. They are typically made up of two or three words but can be longer phrases. Longer terms are referred to as long-tail keywords. Long-tail keywords are more specific and are often less competitive.

Why are keywords important?

When you enter a search query into a search engine like Google, the search engine will crawl web pages to find the closest match.

If your web page includes keywords that match the search term, then search engines use that as an indicator that your page is relevant. Therefore, using keywords can make it easier for potential customers to find your pages.

There are two types of results that appear in a search; paid ads and organic results. Your page will rank organically if it is deemed relevant to the search. This is the desired result for businesses; ranking organically means you don't have to pay for ads.

The more relevant a search engine decides your page is, the higher it will rank on the search results page. Pages that rank on the first page of search results get the most clicks. The higher you are on the results page, the more visitors you are likely to get.

How to choose keywords

It is very difficult to rank highly for the most popular search terms, especially if your website is new or does not have much content. Instead, you should choose long-tail keywords and very specific terms.

Think about the type of language your target audience would use rather than using the technical terminology used within your industry.

There are many free and paid tools available to help you select the right keywords. There are also companies who can do this for you if you are interested in paying to improve your SEO.

If you are just starting out in blogging, then you don't need to be too concerned about keywords; focus on creating quality content that people want to read. Your blog posts will likely include relevant keywords naturally as you will be blogging about subjects relating to your industry.

Including keywords in your blog

It's important not to stuff your blog post full of keywords, but there are some places where you can include them to optimise your content for search engines. These include the headline, first paragraph and a subheading. You should also use keywords in your image alt tags if relevant.

Although keywords are important, you should write for the reader first. If you choose the right topics then keywords will naturally fit into the copy without you having to force them in. This makes your blog more reader-friendly.

If readers feel like you are writing for them and not just the search engines, they are more likely to subscribe. Plus, search engines don't like companies who try and manipulate search results; they will penalise your pages if they think you are doing this.

> **Bonus Tip**
>
> *Use the auto-complete search function on Google to find out what people are searching. This can help you choose long-tailed keywords, headlines and even sub-headings for your blog posts.*

K is for Keywords: chapter takeaways

- ➡ Keywords can help you appear higher in search results

- ➡ Long-tail keywords are more specific and less competitive

- ➡ Do some keyword research to find out what your target audience is searching for

- ➡ Don't overuse keywords or try and force them into your blog posts as you will put readers off

- ➡ Quality blog posts will include keywords naturally

Related chapters

I is for Images

O is for Optimisation

R is for Research

U is for Uniqueness

Layout

Structure your post to be reader friendly

L is for Layout

Your blog layout is important. If the blog post isn't visually appealing then you can lose visitors before they even read a word.

The way people read from a screen is different to how they read from a page and you need to be aware of this. Reading from a screen is more tiring so readers tend to scan more. Make it easy for readers to skim your blog. Use subheadings, bullet points or text boxes.

Take time to think about the blog layout, particularly the following areas:

Headline
Your blog post should have a title and this should stand out just like a headline in a newspaper or magazine. Your headline will be the thing that grabs a reader's attention, so you need to make it stand out.

Put your headline at the top of your blog post so that readers know what it's about. Include keywords in your headline. Refer to the chapter 'H is for Headlines' earlier in this book for more tips on titles.

Images
Images help visitors understand what your blog post is about without having to read it all. You can use infographics, photographs or illustrations to break up the text and make your post more visually attractive.

You should try and include at least one image on your post even if it is just at the top as a header. Make sure you have the correct permissions or licences to use any images you choose. Refer to the chapter, 'I is for Images' earlier in this book for more information on using images.

Subheadings

Subheadings break up the text. Readers tend to scan a post before they read it in full. The subheadings will tell them if it is worth reading the entire text and help them pick out the key points. Try and include keywords in some of your subheadings as this can help with SEO. Make your subheadings stand out by bolding them or making them bigger than the main text.

Capital letters

When we read, our brain recognises the shapes the letters make. Capital letters break this flow and slow our reading down. Capitalising entire words or phrases can look like YOU ARE SHOUTING AT THE READER so avoid doing it.

Don't overuse capital letters and make sure you are consistent. If you use a capital letter for every word in one subheading then do it in all the subheadings.

Background

If you are using a background colour, image or pattern for your blog post then you need to make sure that the text is visible over the top.

Light text on a light background or dark text on a dark background will not be easy for a reader to read and they will probably give up.

Font

Don't use too many different fonts in your post as this

can look messy and confusing. Sans-serif fonts are more popular for online text; evidence suggests they are easier to read on a screen whereas serif fonts are better for print. Use larger fonts for subheadings and titles.

Break up text blocks

Big blocks of text put readers off. Break your text up into paragraphs and leave plenty of white space between the different elements. This makes your post look more attractive and is easier for the reader to identify the different sections.

Make key points stand out

> If a reader is scanning the page, indented paragraphs will indicate that a key point is being presented, because the paragraph stands out from the main text.

You can make key points in a sentence stand out by using bold text.

Use different coloured text to draw attention to a key point

A sentence in large font in the middle of your post will grab attention

You can also draw attention to a section of text using:

- ➡ Bullet points
- ➡ Subheadings
- ➡ Text boxes
- ➡ "Quotes"

Don't go over the top with bold, large or coloured fonts as it will make your post look messy. Highlight one or two key points that you want to get across to the reader.

Link to other pages
Include links to other blog posts, pages on your site or relevant external websites. Don't just copy entire URLs into your post like this; https://www.makeyourcopycount.com/training-workshops/blogging-for-business/. Instead, include a hyperlink so it doesn't detract from the content.

Don't go overboard

It's important that your blog layout is visually appealing but don't be tempted to go over the top with graphics, images, text boxes, pop-ups and highlighted text. This can put readers off and detract from the actual content. The most important thing is delivering the key messages to the reader. If your content is not useful, engaging or interesting then it doesn't matter how pretty it looks, the readers won't come back.

Bonus Tip

Use bold text for your introductory or concluding paragraphs to make them stand out. If you have a call to action at the end of your post, then highlight this using large, coloured or bold text, to draw the reader's attention.

L is for Layout: chapter takeaways

- A poor layout can put readers off your blog post before they even start reading

- Reading from a screen is more tiring than reading from a page

- Make your post easy to scan using subheadings, bullet points and highlighted sections of text

- Don't go overboard with pop-ups, images, different fonts and lots of colours

- Include at least one image in your post

Related chapters

F is for Format

H is for Headlines

I is for Images

K is for Keywords

Marketing

Promote your blog and get more traffic

M is for Marketing

Marketing your blog is vital if you want to get results. Simply writing a great blog post and publishing it on your website won't get you many readers. You need to let people know it is there.

Fortunately, there are plenty of ways you can promote your blog and many of them are completely free. Here are some of the things you can do to help generate more visitors to your blog:

Optimise

Optimise your blog posts. Ensure that search engines can crawl your website pages so that they index your posts and they get listed in search results. Choose good long-tail keywords and include these strategically. Getting found in search engines helps you generate organic website traffic. Refer to the chapter 'O is for Optimisation' earlier in this book to find out more.

Email and newsletters

Email your contacts when you have published a new blog post to let them know it is there. Send out a regular newsletter letting your clients, suppliers and associates know that you have been sharing useful content.

If your post is short in length, you may decide to include the entire blog post in the email body. For long posts, give a summary or the first paragraph and include a 'read more' link. If you are blogging frequently then you could do a collation of your most recent posts.

Social media

Social media is a fantastic way of promoting your blog,

but you need to make sure that you reach your target audience. Sharing your blog post on the right platforms, at the right times and in the right way needs a bit of planning. Refer to the chapter, 'S is for Sharing' later in this book for more information on social media.

Guest blogging

Guest blogging is another effective way of generating interest in your own blog. Choose companies with a similar target audience to you. By writing a post for their blog, you can tap into their followers and subscribers.

There are many benefits to guest blogging, especially when you are trying to build your following. Refer to the chapter, 'G is for Guest blog' earlier in this book for tips on guest blogging.

Ask for likes and shares

Include a call to action and share buttons on your blog and encourage people to promote it. Ask colleagues, friends and family members to like and share your posts on social media. Not everyone will read your post but the more people that share it, the more awareness there will be of your brand, and the more potential readers you will reach.

Contact influencers

An influencer is someone who can influence the buying decisions or opinions of a target demographic or group of people. Examples include:

- Celebrities who promote a product to their fan base

- Someone who has a column in a newspaper or magazine

- An industry expert who many people trust for advice

- Individuals or companies that have a large social media following

Find influencers on social media or within related industries and ask them to promote or share your blog posts. Make sure that you connect with influencers that have a similar target audience to you for maximum results.

Paid advertising

You may decide that you want to invest in some paid advertising to help with marketing your blog. Options include pay per click advertising (PPC), social media ads or paid outreach. Invest some time doing research before you start spending loads of money on adverts, as you could end up wasting money on the wrong thing and not getting results.

Get subscribers

Marketing your blog effectively will help you attract more readers. Once you have attracted new readers, you want to keep them coming back so you need them to subscribe to your blog. Make sure you give readers the option to subscribe. Collect their email address so you can email them when a new post is published or give them the option to add your site to their RSS feed.

Getting your readers to subscribe to your blog means that you build a following and you can share new content far more easily. Sharing useful content helps you build a relationship with potential new customers and keep existing customers engaged with your brand. The better the relationship you have with your blog subscribers, the more likely you are to increase your sales.

Measure your results

Tracking your results using Google Analytics or using social media insights can help you focus your efforts more effectively. You don't want to spend time marketing your blog in a way that isn't generating any engagement from your target audience. Refer to the chapter, 'A is for Analytics' earlier in this book for more information about measuring your results.

Bonus Tip

Try including a link to your latest blog in your email signature. Everyone you email will get the link and it's far more interesting than just a link to your website homepage.

M is for Marketing; chapter takeaways

- ➡ You need to let people know your blog is there if you want them to read it

- ➡ Optimising your post can help it get found in search engines

- ➡ Social media is a cost-effective way of promoting your content

- ➡ Finding influencers who will share your blog posts helps you reach a larger audience

- ➡ Get people to subscribe to your blog to make it easier for them to receive your content

Related chapters

A is for Analytics

G is for Guest blog

O is for Optimisation

S is for Sharing

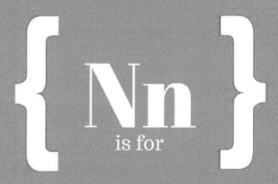

News

Utilise newsjacking, newsletters and industry news

N is for News

'News' is defined by the Oxford dictionary as; "Newly received or noteworthy information, especially about recent events".

The news is a fantastic source of ideas for blog topics and there are many ways in which you can incorporate news into your blog.

Types of news

There are plenty of types of news that bloggers can utilise:

- Company
- Industry
- Local
- Regional
- Nationwide
- Global
- Celebrity
- Financial

- Business
- Political
- Environmental
- Music, film & TV
- Sporting
- Property
- Legal
- Travel

Choose news stories that relate to your business and that will be interesting to your target audience. Here are some ideas of how to blog around news:

Company news
Blogs are a good place to share any company news. If you have developed a new product or service, taken on

a new employee or had a major change to your business, create a blog post around the story.

Sharing company news is a great way to build relationships with customers and potential customers because it gives them an insight into your business.

Industry news
Sharing industry news is a fantastic way of showing your readers that you keep up to date with the latest developments. If the news is particularly complex, you can explain it in a way that your readers will understand. You can also add your own insights on the news which shows your expertise in your field.

Newsjacking
Newsjacking is a term used when you take a breaking news story and create content around it. This is very popular in marketing, especially since the rise of social media.

If you can relate a story back to a product or service, then you can capitalise on news whilst it's generating interest. Newsjacking is very beneficial when done effectively. You need to be quick off the mark to be effective, so you must be up to date with the latest news and be able to put content together fast.

Ongoing stories
With new stories breaking every minute, many stories are quickly forgotten about. If you want to benefit from these then you need to be fast.

However, there are some stories that stay in the news longer and these can be great for bloggers.

Examples include changes to law, reforms or regulations, political matters and even reality TV shows that run over several weeks.

Future events
Keep on top of the latest news announcements so you can plan blogs around upcoming events that will feature heavily in the news.

Researching, planning and writing in advance, means that you don't have to try and generate content in a rush when the event comes around.

Give yourself plenty of time to come up with unique ways of tying your products and services into an event. Look out and plan for the following:

- Celebrity and royal engagement announcements- plan content to go out at the time of the wedding

- Celebrity and royal pregnancy announcements- plan content to go out around the birth

- World Cup/Olympic bids- plan content for when results are announced

- Capital of culture- plan content to go out for when a particular city is the designated city

- Changes to laws- have content ready for when they come into effect

- Elections/referendums- have content prepared for all the possible outcomes

Newsletters

You can adapt news posts into articles for a company newsletter. Alternatively, collating your blog posts as a newsletter and sending it out by email can be a great way of marketing your blog.

Keep it relevant

The most important thing to remember when using news stories as subjects for your blog posts is to make sure they are relevant to your target audience. The blog posts you write must be interesting to your readers or they won't want to read it or subscribe to your blog.

Check your facts

News stories break fast and there are also many occasions where fake news is reported. Make sure you do your research, use trusted sources of information, verify facts and report accurately. If you misinform your customers, then you could end up losing their trust and their business.

Bonus Tip

Use news from the past to create interesting blog posts. You can write a post around anniversaries of important historical events and how they impacted your industry. What was happening in the news around your industry 10, 50 or 100 years ago.

N is for News: chapter takeaways

➡ News is great for finding blog ideas

➡ There are different types of news including company, industry, regional or global

➡ Newsjacking is a good way of using news for marketing purposes but you must be quick

➡ Make sure that you use news that is relevant to your target audience

➡ Always do your research and check facts before reporting on any news

Related chapters

D is for Direction

J is for Journalism

R is for Research

T is for Target audience

Optimisation

Optimise your posts for search engines
and readers

O is for Optimisation

When we enter a search into Google, Bing, Yahoo! or any other search engine, they crawl the internet to find the web pages that are most relevant.

Search engine optimisation (SEO) is the process of enabling search engines to better understand what your web page is about so that they can decide where to rank it in searches.

You can optimise your blog posts to help your target audience find them.

Most people click on pages that appear on the first page of search results. Getting more clicks means getting more website visitors so getting on page one is extremely desirable. Google is the most popular search engine and the one where people want to rank highest.

SEO is a complex subject; this is mainly because nobody knows for sure exactly how the algorithms work. Google is constantly updating the way it ranks pages to ensure that it consistently provides users with the most relevant search results. If it provides results that are not relevant, then users will start to move to other search engines. Google keeps its algorithms secret so that people don't try and manipulate results.

Helping search engines understand what your content is about, makes it easier for them to determine how relevant your post is. Here are some ways you can optimise your blog post:

Keywords

Search engines will crawl the text on your page and pick out words that match the search terms entered. You can optimise your blog post with the keywords you want to be ranked for.

This doesn't mean you should stick keywords into your blog post as many times as you can. Readers don't like this as your post won't make much sense. On top of that, search engines will penalise you for trying to play the system. You need to choose keywords that are relevant to your content and that people will be searching. Use your keywords tactically.

Headlines

Optimise your headline by including a keyword and making it clear what your post is about. Think about what people would be searching when you choose your headline; your headline could be an exact match. For example, if you were looking for ideas for a blog you might type; "What should I blog about?" and this could easily be a blog post title.

URL

URL stands for Uniform Resource Locator and is your webpage address. You can optimise the URL for your blog post by including keywords. When your web page appears in search results the URL is displayed.

Make Your Copy Count: Copywriting Services | Content Writing
https://www.makeyourcopycount.com/ ▼
Great copy is engaging, clear and concise. Communicate your message effectively with **Make Your Copy Count**. Writing. Editing. Training.

Meta descriptions

A meta description is the short bit of copy that appears under your headline and URL in a search result:

Make Your Copy Count: Copywriting Services | Content Writing
https://www.makeyourcopycount.com/ ▼
Great copy is engaging, clear and concise. Communicate your message effectively with **Make Your Copy Count**. Writing. Editing. Training.

You can optimise your meta description by including keywords and a good summary of what your web page or blog post is about.

Alt tags

Alt tags are the description you give to an image. If a visually impaired person is using a screen reader on your site, it will read this description out to them. If your image doesn't load, then it will be replaced with the description from your alt tag.

Make sure that you give your images descriptions as the search engines will crawl these and this will be taken into consideration when deciding how relevant your page is. Leaving them blank is a missed opportunity to optimise your blog.

XML Sitemap

Adding an XML sitemap to your website can make it easier for search engines to crawl your site and index the pages. Refer to the chapter, 'X is for XML sitemap' later in this book for more information.

Yoast

Yoast is considered the most comprehensive SEO plugin for WordPress users. It uses a traffic light system to indicate how optimised your post is for search engines based on your main keyword. It also lets you know how optimised your blog post is for readers by scoring your post for readability based on several factors.

If you are creating blogs in WordPress, then Yoast is a fantastic tool for improving your SEO. Refer to the chapter, 'Y is for Yoast' later in this book for more information.

Linking

Backlinks to and from your website are good for SEO, provided they are quality links. This means not linking to spam sites. Refer to the chapter, 'B is for Backlinks' earlier in this book for more information about backlinks.

You should also link internal pages on your site. This not only helps the reader navigate your site more easily but it helps search engines crawl and index your site faster.

Add content regularly

Search engines constantly crawl the internet looking for new content. If they see that you are adding new content to your site regularly they will reward that. It shows that your site is still active and that you are sharing useful content. The more pages you have, the more opportunities there are to rank in search results so the more chance there is of reaching your target audience. The more traffic you get, the more search engines will view your pages as relevant.

Optimise for readers

Getting found in search engines is important so you do need to think about SEO when you write your blog posts, but don't forget about your readers. There is no point being ranked number one in search results if your readers aren't interested in reading your post.

The best way to naturally optimise your site is to create content that is useful, engaging and interesting for your target audience. If you choose subjects for blog posts that are related to your industry, you will naturally include keywords in the copy. If you use pictures that are relevant to the post you are writing, then the descriptions will naturally contain keywords.

Choose the topics your target audience want to read about and then market your blog effectively. Sharing your blog on social media is a great way to get more traffic. More traffic will help boost your SEO which will, in turn, get you more traffic. If you are creating great content, then it should be easier to optimise your blog.

Bonus Tip

Use tags and hashtags to optimise your posts on social media sites. Hashtags are like keywords and make it easier for users to find your content. There are apps available to help you find the best hashtags.

#bloggingtips

O is for Optimisation: chapter takeaways

➡ Search engine optimisation (SEO) is the process of making it easy for search engines to understand what your blog post or web page is about

➡ Consider the following things before publishing a new post

  o Choose relevant keywords

  o Optimise your headline

  o Optimise your meta data

  o Check your image alt tags

  o Include internal links

➡ Make sure your post is optimised for readers too

Related chapters

  B is for Backlinks

  Q is for Quantity

  X is for XML Sitemap

  Y is for Yoast

{ **Pp** }

is for

Proofreading

Eliminate spelling and punctuation errors

P is for Proofreading

Proofreading your blog post before it goes live is extremely important. You don't want all the hard work you have put into the researching, writing and editing to be let down by a stray apostrophe or accidental typo. There are a number of reasons why you should do a thorough proofread of any copy before you publish it:

Errors can change the meaning
Incorrect punctuation or spelling can completely change the meaning of your copy, as in these examples:

Woman: without her, man is nothing

Woman, without her man, is nothing

The doctor had no patients

The doctor had no patience

Errors can put readers off
Readers may forgive the odd mistake here and there, but if your copy is littered with spelling mistakes, grammatical errors and incorrect punctuation, then it will put readers off. Your copy will be too hard to follow and if you can't put the effort into checking it, why should readers put the effort into trying to decipher it?

Errors can disrupt the flow of your copy
Have you ever had have been reading and then had to go back and go back to it and read it again because something didn't make sense?

Even small mistakes, like the ones in the above sentence,

can break the flow which causes frustration for the reader.

Errors can detract from the content
Unfortunately, many people tend to focus on the negative. You could create the most engaging, informative, interesting blog post ever written but if it is full of errors, then that's what readers will pick up on. Make sure your content is remembered for the right reasons.

Common mistakes

Watch out for these common mistakes when you're proofreading your blog post.

Typos
Whether you're inexperienced at typing or type at speed, it's all too easy to hit the wrong key or hit them in the wrong order. Don't rely on a spell check tool to pick up on typos. Typing 'form' instead of 'from', 'fiend' instead of 'friend' or 'manger' instead of 'manager' can easily slip through unnoticed.

Apostrophes
Lots of people find apostrophes confusing and the rules aren't always straightforward. However, it is beneficial to remember these two main uses:

1. When there is a letter or letters missing, usually when two words have been merged together, the apostrophe replaces the missing letter.

   For example; don't (do + not), you're (you + are) he's (he + is)

2. When you're indicating that something belongs to a thing or person.

   For example; "it was his **sister's** car" (the car belongs to his sister), "it was her **friend's** birthday" (the birthday belongs to her friend) or "he could hear the **car's** engine" (the engine belongs to the car).

When you're adding the letter 's' to a word to turn it into a plural, you do not need an apostrophe.

For example, "he had three sisters", "many of her friends would be there", "the showroom was full of classic cars".

Homophones
Homophones are words that sound the same when spoken but are spelt differently and have different meanings. They catch a lot of people out. Some commonly confused ones are:

- Affect/effect
- Allowed/aloud
- Bear/bare
- Complement/compliment
- Dual/duel
- Hear/here
- Heel/heal
- Hire/higher
- Hole/whole

- New/knew
- Lose/loose
- Past/passed
- Patients/patience
- Plane/plain
- Practice/practise
- Principal/principle
- Sale/sail
- Sea/see
- Site/sight
- Stationery/stationary
- There/their/they're
- To/too/two
- Where/wear
- Whether/weather
- Which/witch
- Write/right/rite
- Your/you're

Local dialect
In some regions, the local accent means some words are pronounced in a way that sounds like other words and this can cause confusion when they are being written. Examples include;

- 'Are' instead of 'our'
- 'Been' instead of 'being'
- 'Seen' instead of 'seeing'

If this applies to you, then you should be mindful of using the correct words in your blog. Also try and steer clear of using local slang as readers from other areas may not understand it.

'Of' instead of 'have'
A common mistake is using the word 'of'' instead of 'have'. Many people say, "should of", "would of" or "could of" instead of "should have", "would have" or "could have". You should always use 'have' because 'of' is not grammatically correct.

Capitalisation
Capital letters should be used for the first letter of a sentence or subheading. They should also be used for proper nouns (for example, names of people, countries and cities). Acronyms are often capitalised (for example; search engine optimisation= SEO).

Top tips for proofreading your blog post

Leave your copy overnight
There are three stages to your blog writing process. The first stage is to write your post, the second is to edit and the third is to proofread. You should leave at least one day between each stage as then you are going back to it with fresh eyes and are more likely to spot mistakes.

Read out loud
Reading your post out loud will help you identify

mistakes more easily. You will notice any awkward sentence structure, grammatical errors and missing words. If you have software that has a 'read aloud' function then this can be very useful for checking your content.

Get a fresh pair of eyes
Get a friend or colleague to give your blog post a final check before you publish it. They will be more likely to spot mistakes as it will be the first time they have read the post. Alternatively, you could hire a proofreader who will check your work thoroughly.

Use grammar checking software
Software like Grammarly is very useful for picking up errors in your work. It shouldn't be used as a substitute for manual proofreading but it provides an extra check.

Check it again in context
Once you have put your blog post together and are ready to publish, give it one last proofread in context. Sometimes seeing it alongside the images and on the page as it would be seen by readers can help you spot bits that don't quite work.

Bonus Tip

Identify what your common mistakes are. Which words do you struggle to spell, get confused with or overuse? Make a list of your common mistakes and make a conscious effort to double check those words in every blog post.

P is for Proofreading: chapter takeaways

➡ You should always proofread your blog post thoroughly before publishing

➡ Familiarise yourself with basic grammar and punctuation rules

➡ Watch out for commonly confused words

➡ Reading your copy out loud makes it easier to identify mistakes

➡ Use grammar checking software as a back-up

Related chapters

E is for Editing

J is for Journalism

R is for Research

W is for Writing

{ Qq } is for

Quantity

Consider the frequency and word counts of your posts

Q is for Quantity

"How often should you blog?" and "How long should a blog post be?" are common questions.

There is no right or wrong answer because it depends on several factors. Here are some things you need to consider before you decide on the right answers for you:

Frequency

How much time can you dedicate?
Blogging takes time. You need to plan, research, write, edit and proofread your post. On top of that, there's the time it takes to promote and share your posts. Before you commit to a daily, weekly or fortnightly blog, make sure you have enough time to dedicate to it. You might find it more manageable to create one in-depth, high-quality post each month rather than trying to create something every day.

How fast-paced is your industry?
If you are in a fast-moving industry then you may need to blog more frequently to keep your readers up to date. Daily posts or weekly round-ups of the latest developments could work well.

How in-depth are your posts?
The length of your posts can dictate how often you blog. If you are writing short, snappy posts then you might find it realistic to write a post every day. Longer more in-depth or ultimate guides will take a bit longer to create so you might prefer to post these less frequently. Having a mixture of content length is another option. A short weekly blog and one long post each month or a short

monthly post with a long, in-depth post every quarter can be a nice combination.

What do you want to achieve from your blog?
The purpose of your blog can determine how often you need to blog. The more frequent your posts, the better it is for SEO as you'll be adding consistent content. Creating blogs regularly can help build brand awareness and increase your social media following. However, if you want to be viewed as an industry expert you might prefer to create long, detailed posts that are less frequent but attract a good readership.

Length

Posts less than 300 words don't really give search engines enough content to determine how relevant your post is.

Longer posts of over 1000 words rank higher than shorter posts. This is usually because you automatically include your keyword and variations of your keywords more naturally so search engines can determine more from the copy. There isn't really a limit on how many words you can write, but you need to have good writing skills and a strong subject to keep your reader engaged for over 1500 words.

If you are creating long posts then you need to think carefully about the layout. Include plenty of subheadings, images or graphics to make it more visually appealing.

The format of your post may determine the length of your post. If your post is a "quick guide" to something then readers will expect it to be short. If you are creating an "ultimate guide" then readers will expect plenty of information.

The key thing to remember is to write enough to comprehensively cover your chosen topic but don't waffle.

Go for quality over quantity

Don't write blog posts for the sake of having a blog post and don't add paragraphs of content purely to make up a long word count.

You should always aim for quality over quantity. Readers will be more likely to read, subscribe and share if they feel that they are getting something high-quality.

Bonus Tip

If you choose a subject that is in-depth and your post begins to run into 2000 words, then split it into a two or three-part post. This will give readers a reason to come back after part one and they will spend more time on your site and visit more pages which is good for SEO.

Q is for Quantity: chapter takeaways

➡ You need to consider these things before deciding how often you should blog:

- o How much time can you dedicate to blogging?

- o How fast paced is your industry?

- o What length are your posts?

- o What do you want to achieve from your blog?

➡ The length of your post should be over 300 words

➡ Longer posts get ranked higher in search results

➡ Go for quality over quantity

Related chapters

D is for Direction

F is for Format

M is for Marketing

O is for Optimisation

Research

Make sure you research you topic

R is for Research

Carrying out thorough research ensures that you have an accurate blog post and the content is interesting and useful to the reader.

The more facts, statistics and new information you can offer compared to competitors, the more likely you are to win a bigger readership.

Even if you know your subject inside out, it pays to research facts and figures to make sure the information you give is up to date and correct.

If you misquote a source or give incorrect information, you could open yourself up to problems. Depending on your industry, you could be breaking industry regulations or failing compliance.

If you have written something about someone that is false and perceived as damaging to their reputation, you could be accused of defamation and get caught up on libel charges.

Top tips for effective research

Plan your research before you start
Ask yourself what questions you want answering. Have a clear plan for the information you need to find so you keep your research on track.

Industry news subscriptions
Subscribe to websites, newsletters and blogs that provide useful information about your industry.

Magazines and books

Magazines and books around your chosen subjects provide a wealth of information. You can pick the most relevant sections and use the information for your blog.

Google

Online searches are a quick and easy way to get the information you need. Just be wary of the sources as not everything on the internet is true. If you aren't using a reputable source, then verify your findings with other sites to make sure your information is correct.

Government websites

Government websites are reputable sources of information. If you need to research laws and legislation then government websites are a great place to start.

Conduct surveys

If you want to write a unique blog post about your subject, then you can conduct your own surveys or market research and use these findings in your post.

Academic reports

There are a wealth of academic research papers and reports available to draw information from for your blog posts. You can use Google Scholar to search published papers online.

Interviews

Conduct interviews with experts on the subject you are writing about. They can provide unique insights and add extra credibility to your blog post. Refer to the chapter 'J is for Journalism' earlier in this book for tips on conducting effective interviews.

Other people's research and studies

You can use papers and research findings from other companies if you reference your source. The easiest way to do this is to include a hyperlink back to the original source.

Stay on track

It can be very easy to get distracted when researching. If you come across interesting materials that aren't related to the subject you are writing about, bookmark them and go back to them at a later stage.

Don't let yourself go off on a tangent with your research otherwise, you may spend hours reading and be no closer to writing your post. If you want to research effectively, you need to stay on track.

How to use your research

Present information clearly

Put information in a way that makes sense and that is accessible to your target audience. If your subject is complex and you are trying to simplify it for your audience, use concise language. Analogies can also be an effective way of explaining something.

Make sure it is accurate

Check your facts before you publish. There are several websites that allow you to check your information is accurate:

- ➡ FullFact.org
- ➡ FactCheck.org
- ➡ Checkdesk.org

Link to sources when necessary
If you are using somebody else's research or quoting a source then you should attribute correctly. Hyperlinks are the easiest way to reference your source as the reader can click straight through.

Make your blog post unique
Don't just repeat information you have found. Present it in a new and interesting way. Put your own spin on the topic or get experts to give their views and insights.

Bonus Tip

Build yourself a knowledge database as you research. Bookmark interesting online articles and websites that you can use in later blog posts. Put together a file or scrapbook of useful articles you find in magazines or photocopy useful pages from books. You will start to grow your own library of information to draw on. If you come across an article that may be useful in the future you can save it rather than having to try and search for it again months later. You can even use some of the saved information as inspiration for new blog post ideas.

R is for Research: chapter takeaways

➡ Well-researched blog posts will be more interesting and useful to readers

➡ Plan your research in advance to help you stay on track

➡ Check your facts are correct before using them in your blog

➡ Present your research in a clear way and cite sources when necessary

➡ Try and present your research in a unique way

Related chapters

F is for Format

J is for Journalism

U is for Uniqueness

W is for Writing

{ Ss }
is for

Sharing

Share your posts in the right places

S is for Sharing

Sharing your blog posts on social media is an excellent way of generating new readers and building brand awareness. Choose the right platforms, post at the right times and engage with the right audience for better results.

Which platforms should you use?

There are so many social media platforms available it can be hard to choose the right ones. Managing a social media account successfully takes time and effort. You need to update, share and engage with your audience regularly.

If you do not have a dedicated social media or marketing person, then choose just one or two platforms. Doing one or two well is better than trying to be on every platform and not engaging with your followers effectively.

Here are some of the most popular platforms:

Facebook
Facebook has the most users of any social media channel. You can build a business page where you can share your blog posts and any other content. You can also create paid ads on Facebook to help you reach your target audience more effectively.

Twitter
Twitter is a fast-paced platform. You share 'Tweets' which anyone can see; 'Tweets' are short posts and can include links to your blog. Users can follow people whose

posts they want to see more of. You can follow anyone on Twitter and they can follow you back if they choose.

LinkedIn

LinkedIn is a business and employment-related social media platform. If you offer business to business products and services then LinkedIn is a good platform for you.

Pinterest

Pinterest allows you to create 'boards' where you pin posts, images and other media content. You can share your boards and allow anyone to view your pinned content.

Instagram

Instagram is a very visual platform. Anyone can follow you and find your images. Use hashtags to make it easier for people to find your content. If you have a visual product or service then Instagram is a good platform for you.

YouTube

YouTube is a video sharing platform. If you are including video on your blog posts then embed the YouTube link into your blog and include links to your blog posts on your YouTube channel

Feedly

Feedly is a news aggregator app. Choose subjects you are interested in and you will get a feed of blogs and articles related to that subject. Feedly is a good tool for finding content to share with your audience and researching for your own blog.

Medium

Medium is a free platform where you can share blogs and articles. Blogs that get more likes and comments appear higher in feeds so the quality of your blog post is important.

Tumblr

Tumblr is a micro-blogging site where users can share media in short blog posts. Users can follow other users' blogs. You can add tags to your posts to make them easier to find.

Reddit

Reddit is another social news aggregator. You can share links or text posts. Registered users vote submissions up or down which determines where your posts appear in a feed.

Snapchat

Snapchat is a mobile app that allows you to share photos and videos with your audience. The images and videos 'self-destruct' once viewed.

Which is right for you?

With so many social media platforms available, it can be difficult to choose the best one. We suggest choosing the platform that your target audience is using.

If you are looking for a younger audience, then Instagram or Snapchat might work for you. If you are a business to business company, then LinkedIn is a good platform.

How often should you post?

The number of times you share your posts will depend on the platform you are using. On Twitter, it is more acceptable to share the same post several times whereas, LinkedIn users would not appreciate you saturating their feed with the same post repeatedly.

The key thing to remember is to share a combination of your own content and other people's content.

When should you post?

Think about when your target audience is going to be online. Sharing your blog post in the middle of the night when your readers are in bed won't be very effective. If you are targeting business owners, then Monday mornings when they have just got back to their desk might not be the best time. If you are writing for students then evening and weekends might be a good time to post.

Using images

Including an image makes your post stand out more in social media feeds. On more visual platforms like Instagram and Snapchat, an image is essential. Make sure you use original images or images that you have the correct permissions or licences to use. Refer to the chapter 'I is for Images' earlier in this book for more details on image copyright and free images.

Share buttons

Make sure that you have share buttons somewhere in your post. This allows readers to quickly share your post on their social media pages. They can share your post even if you don't have a profile on that platform.

Automation

You can automate the sharing of your blog posts using apps like 'Hootsuite' which allow you to write your social media posts in advance and schedule when you want to publish them. You can schedule all your posts for the day or week ahead, saving you time and making sure you don't miss key sharing opportunities.

Tracking results

Use your social media analytics and Google Analytics_ to track which posts are getting the most engagement. This allows you to see which blog posts get the most click-throughs and which social media platforms are driving the most visitors to your site, so you can market your blog more effectively. Refer to the chapter 'A is for Analytics' earlier in this book for more on measuring results.

Influencer marketing

Influencer marketing is a way of reaching a bigger audience. Find people or companies that share your target audience and ask them to promote your blog posts on their social media channels. By getting them to share your content, you widen your reach.

Other ways of sharing your blog post

Social media is a fantastic way of sharing your blog for free, but there are other ways to market your blog too. Share via email newsletters, join blogging communities or use paid advertising. Refer to the chapter 'M is for Marketing' earlier in this book for more ways to market your blog.

> ### *Bonus Tip*
>
> *When you share your post on social media, change the copy in the summary of your post. This keeps it fresh; different words will attract different people.*
>
> *For example, if you are sharing a blog on finding blog topics, you could use the following:*
>
> *"Check out our latest blog post on how to generate original ideas for your blog"*
>
> *"Do you struggle to come up with ideas for your blog? Check out our top tips here"*
>
> *"We're sharing our top tips on how to find ideas for a unique blog post topic"*
>
> *"Looking for inspiration for your next blog post? Check out our expert advice"*
>
> *"Banish boring blogs with our top tips for unique blog ideas"*

S is for Sharing: chapter takeaways

- Using one or two social media platforms effectively is better than trying to spread your time across all of them

- Use the platforms your target audience are using

- Think about the times that your readers will be online

- Track your results to make sure you're sharing in the right place

- Include share buttons on your blog posts so readers can share on their social media pages

Related chapters

A is for Analytics

H is for Headlines

I is for Images

M is for Marketing

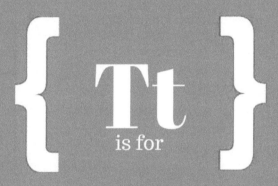

{ **Tt** }
is for

Target audience

Identify who you want to reach

T is for Target audience

Understanding your target audience is absolutely vital if you want a successful blog. If you don't know who your target audience is, how can you know what they want to read about?

Identifying exactly who you are trying to reach through your blog will help you generate blog ideas, find more readers and build a stronger following.

Identifying your target audience

The target audience for your blog may be more specific than the target audience for your products. You have to consider who you can actually reach with your blog. If you sell to all sizes of business, then it may be easier to reach small business owners with your blog than CEOs of international companies.

If you have multiple target audiences then you may decide just to focus on one. For example, a recruitment company wants to attract high-quality candidates but they also need to attract employers who want to recruit. They could focus their blog on attracting more candidates, writing about what to wear to an interview or what to include in a CV. Alternatively, they may choose to focus on employers and create blogs around conducting effective telephone interviews or making a job offer.

Before you write each blog post, decide who you are writing for.

Business to business

If you offer business to business products or services, then consider the following about your audience:

- What size company are they?

- How many employees do they have?

- What is the average turnover?

- Are they start-ups, SMEs or corporates?

- Is location important?

- Are they a specific type of business (i.e. solicitors)?

- Do they work in a particular sector (i.e. construction)?

- Who are their clients?

Business to consumer

If you sell products or services directly to consumers, then consider the following about your target audience:

- Are they male or female?

- What age are they?

- Is location important?

- What kind of income do they have?

- Are they homeowners?

- Do they have children?

- What is their marital status?

- Are they drivers?

- Do they own a specific item (i.e. car)?

- Do they have a specific hobby (i.e. gardening)?

Once you have identified your target audience, you can determine some further information.

- What problems do they come across in their day-to-day lives or careers?

- What are their buying habits?

- Have they got particular likes or dislikes, hobbies or interests?

All these factors can help you make decisions about the type of post you are going to write and the subjects you are going to blog about.

Finding and engaging your target audience

Knowing as much information as possible about your target audience can help you understand where to find them.

You can research which social media platforms your target audience use most, which websites they visit most often and the times of day they are online. Use this information to market your blog more effectively.

If you have taken time to understand your target audience then this will come across in your blog. You will be able to write directly to your audience and answer their questions. Readers will be able to relate to your posts and this will help you create a more loyal following and build better relationships.

T is for Target audience: chapter takeaways

➡ Understanding your target audience helps you
create better blog posts

➡ Identify who you are writing to before every blog
post

➡ Build a profile of your target audience- who is your
ideal reader?

➡ Think about where you can reach your target
audience so you can market your blog more
effectively

➡ Write for your target audience about subjects they
are interested in and use language they understand

Related chapters

D is for Direction

M is for Marketing

S is for Sharing

W is for Writing

Uniqueness

Make your blog stand out from the crowd

U is for Uniqueness

It can be hard to make your blog stand out. Those in niche markets often struggle to think of subjects to blog about, whereas those from saturated markets feel like there are no original topics left.

Creating a unique blog doesn't necessarily mean you have to have a unique idea. It just means you need to present your idea in a unique way.

Controversial
Can you make your blog unique by being controversial? Do you have a differing view to that of your competitors about a new industry development? Maybe you offer a totally honest and open narrative in a sector that is often under scrutiny or suspicion. Are you willing to discuss the issues that your competitors avoid, or address common myths or misconceptions about your industry?

Extra detail
Make posts about common topics stand out by providing extra details, additional advice or more in-depth analysis than competitors. This may involve extra research but will give your readers a more comprehensive understanding of the subject and show that you care about providing useful content.

Personal opinion
Put some of your personality into your blog posts by offering your own personal opinions on a subject. Instead of sticking to a factual review, include your own experiences, real-world examples and stories.

Unique point of view

Offer a unique point of view on a subject. That could be your own point of view or that of an industry expert. If there is a change to legislation, interview someone who has been directly affected by the change. Get guest bloggers to write posts to give your readers a change. Write your posts as if from the point of view of a fictional character, child, animal or product to give your blog a twist.

Use analogies

Analogies are a great way of explaining things that are boring, complex or difficult in a way that readers can understand. They bring subjects to life by giving readers something they can visualise or relate to. You can also use analogies to give a fresh perspective on subjects that have already been covered in detail.

New research

Make your blog post unique by including new research findings. This could be research you have carried out yourself through interviews and surveys or someone else's research presented in an original way.

Unique style

The tone of your blog posts could be what makes them unique. If your blog posts are funnier or more entertaining than similar blogs in your industry, then you will attract more readers because you are offering something different.

Dare to be different

It doesn't matter what industry you work in, you can be creative with your blog. As long as the information is not misleading or defamatory, you can present it in a way that appeals to your target audience and makes you stand out.

U is for Uniqueness: chapter takeaways

➡ Make your blog stand out by being different to your competitors

➡ You can make your blog different by:

- ○ Being controversial

- ○ Offering more in-depth information

- ○ Writing from a unique point of view

- ○ Using new research

- ○ Adding your personal opinion

- ○ Using analogies

- ○ Writing in a unique style

➡ Present information in a way that appeals to your audience and make sure it is accurate

Related chapters

F is for Format

G is for Guest blog

J is for Journalism

R is for Research

Video

Try adding some videos to your blog to keep it fresh

V is for Video

Including video on your blog is a great way of making your blog stand out. Videos are excellent for sharing on social media and they engage a bigger audience than text-only posts. Blogs containing video content generate more backlinks than those without so they can help with your SEO too.

You can do video only blogs (vlogs) to post on a video sharing platform such as YouTube or Vimeo, or to share on your website. However, combining video and text provides more benefits than just using text or video alone.

Use video and text

Having both video and text means you cater to a bigger audience. You appeal to people who find it easier to take information in from watching and listening, as well as people who take information in through reading. If someone clicks on your post and the video is not working or they don't want the sound on, they can still read the text. If someone does not like reading they can just watch the video. You're offering the best of both worlds.

You don't have to include a video with every blog post but adding a video every now and then keeps your blog fresh and interesting.

Ideas for video content

Presentations
If you have delivered a presentation, workshop or

training course, then why not repurpose the slides by turning them into a video presentation.

You can use PowerPoint to turn your presentations into a video by adding a voiceover to your slides. This can then be uploaded to YouTube or other similar video sharing platforms.

To turn your PowerPoint presentation into a video, open the file, click on 'Slide Show' and then click on 'Record Slide Show' and start recording your video.

Save your completed video and upload it to YouTube. You can then embed the video into your blog.

Interviews
Interviews make good videos. It can be useful to let the interviewee know the questions in advance if they are not used to being filmed. This allows them to prepare so there aren't long pauses and they give more structured answers. Refer to the chapter 'J is for Journalism' earlier in this book for top tips on conducting interviews.

Case studies
Filming before and after footage or creating time-lapse videos of your projects is a fantastic way of showcasing your services.

How-to
Explainer videos are very popular. Show your client or customers how to do something or how to use something in a step-by-step video.

Reviews
Videos showing you using products and reviewing them

as you go makes your reviews stand out. Customers can see the results for themselves so they get a more comprehensive view of the product.

Top tips
Create short, snappy videos sharing your top tips on a particular subject. Just a short one-minute video saying what the tip is will attract viewers interested in that subject. You can create a whole series using a different tip for each blog.

Testimonials
Video testimonials can be created to add weight to claims about a particular product or service you offer. They show that you are credible. You can add them to blog posts that relate to that part of your business.

Creating videos

Filming
Creating a video doesn't have to be difficult or expensive. Most mobile phones and smart devices have a built-in camera allowing you to make basic videos. You can purchase tripods and microphones for a small cost to enhance your mobile videos.

Webcams for laptops, Macs and PCs are another option. These are great if you are just creating a short video where you are talking directly to the camera.

Most digital cameras also have a video option and depending on the quality of your camera, you can create high-resolution or HD videos. Again, you can buy tripods, microphones and other accessories to improve your video.

Go-pro cameras are great for filming active videos; running, cycling, climbing, skiing etc.

For a professionally filmed video, there are many excellent videographers and production companies that can help depending on whether you want live video, studio shot footage or animated video.

Editing

There are hundreds of options for video editing software, some free and some paid depending on what level of editing you need. Many of them offer a free trial that you can download straight from their site to start using straight away.

If you would prefer to get your videos filmed and edited by a professional videographer or production company then do a bit of research to find a company whose style you like.

Sharing

You can upload your videos to your Facebook page, YouTube, Vimeo and many other platforms. They can easily be embedded into your blog posts or you can share a link straight to your videos.

Remember your target audience

Videos are an excellent form of content marketing but it is important that you always keep your target audience in mind. What videos are they interested in watching? How will you share your video blog content?

Make sure that the videos you create fit with your blog strategy or overall marketing strategy and don't forget to measure your engagement to make sure you are getting the results you want.

V is for Video: chapter takeaways

➡ Blogs containing both video and text appeal to more people

➡ Ideas for video subjects include:

  o Presentations

  o Interviews

  o Case studies

  o Explainer videos

  o Reviews

  o Top tips

  o Testimonials

➡ Research videographers and production companies to find the best one for your needs

Related chapters

  A is for Analytics

  D is for Direction

  J is for Journalism

  Z is for Zzzz

Writing

Write for your readers

W is for Writing

If you want to build a blog that gets results then you need to write engaging blog posts. There's no point coming up with great ideas and spending hours writing loads of words if nobody is interested in reading what you've written.

Planning and research

Build a brief
It is important that each blog post fits with your overall strategy, but you also need a brief for each individual post.

➡ What is the purpose of your blog post?

➡ Do you want to promote a specific product or service?

➡ Who is your target audience for this specific post?

➡ What action do you want them to take after reading your post?

Building a brief will help you choose your subject.

Generate ideas and choose a format

Come up with a selection of ideas for your posts and decide which will be the most suitable.

See Appendix 3 for tips on generating ideas

Once you've chosen your subject, consider the following:

➡ What problem will your post solve or what question will you answer?

- What questions would your reader have about the subject?

- How can you make your post unique?

- Which formats would work for your chosen subject?

Come up with ideas for headlines based on the subject you have chosen. Decide what format you will use for your post. Do some research on which keywords people are using.

Refer to chapters 'H is for Headlines', 'F is for Format' and 'K is for Keywords' earlier in this book for more help with planning your post.

Research your topic and collate information
Conduct research on your chosen topic to ensure your blog post is accurate and contains useful information. Collate all the information you gather and decide what you will include in your post. Refer to the chapter 'R is for Research' earlier in this book for guidance on research techniques.

Writing your posts

Once you have a general idea of what you want your post to be about and you have done some research, you need to write your post. The hardest part is usually getting started. Once you get going, you find the ideas start to flow more easily. Here are some tips for writing your post:

Set aside time to write
The first thing to do is plan a time where you can

concentrate on writing your post. You may decide to do this outside of normal working hours or quiet times where you won't be distracted by phone calls and emails. Alternatively, switch your phone to silent and close your emails down whilst you write.

Write first and edit later
Don't try and edit your post as you go. Writing the first paragraph will take far longer if you try and make it perfect. Instead, just get your ideas down, no matter how badly written, then go back through and improve it later. Nobody sees your first draft apart from you so it doesn't matter if it isn't any good.

Find your writing style
Some people start by jotting down bullet points and then filling out the information. Some people write their introduction last. Other people just write from start to finish and then reorder the information afterwards. There is no right or wrong way to write; do what works for you.

Write to your reader
Write as though you are talking directly to the reader. Talk about "I", "we" and "you" to make your post more engaging.

Write as though you are having a conversation with your reader. This doesn't mean write how you speak and it doesn't mean using informal language if that doesn't fit with your brand personality. It simply means that you should make your post sound natural.

Avoid long sentences and paragraphs
Improve the flow of your writing by using a combination

of both long and short sentences and paragraphs. Don't let a single sentence go over thirty words. If you find a sentence is over thirty words, remove unnecessary words or split it in two. Sentences of over thirty words are hard to follow as in this example:

If your sentence is really long and covers more than one point then your readers will find it hard to focus on what you are saying and by the time they get to the end of the sentence, they will have forgotten what the original point of the sentence was, so it is better to split long sentences in two and put separate points in separate sentences rather than try and get everything all in one sentence.

Keep paragraphs to a maximum of four or five sentences to avoid big blocks of text.

Think about the structure
Think about the layout of your post. You should use headings and sub-headings to break up the text. Think about what images or videos you will include and how you can incorporate these. Consider what other blog posts or pages on your site you will link back to and how you will fit the links into the copy.

Keep it logical
Keep your ideas in a logical order and stay on track. Don't jump from one point to another and then back to a point that you started out with. You may have to change the order of some of your paragraphs once you've written the post or cut copy out where you have repeated an idea.

Use appropriate language
Don't use industry jargon or technical terminology if

you aren't writing to other people in your industry. Keep your language as simple as possible so that your post is easy to follow.

Avoid offensive terms or words. Use a tone that is suitable for your company whether that is formal, informal or somewhere in between.

End strong
Give your post a strong conclusion and include a call to action rather than just letting it fizzle out. A summary of the points or a paragraph tying it all together is a good way to finish. Refer to chapter 'C is for Call to action' earlier in this book for advice on creating a strong call to action.

Editing & proofreading

Once you have written your blog post leave it overnight (or longer if you can) before going back to edit it. Editing is where you have the chance to perfect your post.

Think about whether you have covered your subject as sufficiently as you could. Is your blog useful, interesting or entertaining? Could you add something else to make it even better? Are there bits you can cut to make it stronger. Refer to the chapter 'E is for Editing' for more tips on editing your blog posts.

Once you have edited your post, leave it again and then give it a final proofread before publishing. This allows you to go back to it with fresh eyes, making it easier to spot mistakes. Refer to the chapter 'P is for Proofreading' for tips on proofreading.

Editing and proofreading your post before you share it ensures a better quality of post than one that you have rushed to get out. Your blog represents the kind of company you are, so make sure it shows you in the best light.

> *Bonus Tip*
>
> *The rule of three:*
>
> *In writing, things that come in threes are, more satisfying, more memorable and more effective.*
>
> *"We save you time, save you money and reduce stress"*
>
> *"Your employees will be more motivated, more engaged and more productive"*
>
> *"The latest version is bigger, stronger and longer-lasting"*

W is for Writing: chapter takeaways

- Plan and research before you start to write anything

- Find your own writing style; there is no right or wrong

- Don't worry about your first draft being perfect; you can edit it at a later stage

- Use appropriate language and terminology for your target audience

- Think about layout and how you can link to other blog posts you have written

Related chapters

E is for Editing

L is for Layout

P is for Proofreading

R is for Research

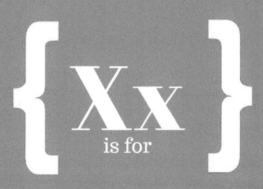

XML sitemap

Make it easier for Google

X is for XML Sitemap

An XML sitemap is like a roadmap of your website for search engines. It helps search engines crawl your site more easily and index the pages. This lets them find new content quicker and makes it easier for them to determine the relevance of your pages in search queries, improving your SEO.

Google likes to understand every page on your site and an XML sitemap makes that easier.

Benefits of an XML Sitemap

A sitemap is useful if your website or blog is new as you won't have built many quality backlinks to aid search engines in discovering the pages. A sitemap helps search engines crawl your site more efficiently.

If you have a website where you have a lot of content, a sitemap improves the visibility of your site by allowing search engines to interact more effectively with your site. The XML sitemap should include modification dates which will tell search engines which pages to crawl and which ones haven't changed.

A sitemap lists all your URLs including the pages that aren't discoverable by search engines or that they might miss when indexing. You can also tell search engines which pages are a priority so they can order the crawling.

Your sitemap can give search engines information about how important a page is in relation to other pages, how often you make changes to your site and when the last update was. An XML sitemap keeps all this information in one place so the search engines can find it easily.

Do you need an XML Sitemap?

You don't necessarily need a sitemap as Google can usually crawl your site if your pages have been properly linked. However, there are some sites that benefit from the addition of a sitemap:

- Sites with complicated structure or lots of pages

- New sites or sites with very few links

- Sites with lots of isolated or archived pages

- Sites using rich media content or dynamic pages

Bonus Tip

If you aren't sure if you have an XML sitemap or whether you need one, don't worry. Think of your site as a big spiderweb. Connect the pages using relevant links. This makes it easier for search engines to crawl your site, but it also helps readers navigate. Guiding the reader from one page to the next keeps them on your site longer and increases your exposure to them. This gives you a greater chance to build relationships and trust.

X is for XML Sitemap: chapter takeaways

- An XML sitemap is like a roadmap of your website for search engines

- A sitemap is useful if your website or blog is new as you won't have built many quality backlinks

- A sitemap helps search engines crawl your site more efficiently

- An XML sitemap keeps information in one place, so the search engines can find it easily

- You don't always need an XML sitemap, especially if pages have been linked correctly

Related chapters

B is for Backlinks

D is for Direction

O is for Optimisation

Y is for Yoast

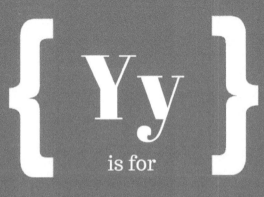

{ Yy }
is for

Yoast

The #1 WordPress SEO plugin

Y is for Yoast

WordPress is one of the most popular platforms for bloggers as it is easy to use and completely customisable using various themes and plugins.

Yoast is a company that specialises in SEO. They developed the WordPress plugin, Yoast SEO, to help WordPress users optimise their web pages more effectively. Yoast SEO is hailed as the world's number one WordPress SEO plugin.

Yoast also offers other WordPress plugins to improve more specific SEO such as local SEO, news SEO, video SEO and E-commerce SEO. As well as their plugins, they also provide online SEO training and other services plus lots of useful articles on various elements of SEO.

Benefits of using Yoast SEO for your blog

Using Yoast SEO for your WordPress blog is beneficial. It helps you identify the areas you need to pay attention to so you can optimise your content. It also lets you know if you have already used a keyword on another page on your site so that you don't duplicate keywords across pages.

SEO Analysis

Yoast SEO works on a traffic light system. Once you have written your post and selected your keyword, Yoast will score your content as red, amber or green. Green means that your post has good optimisation, amber means it is ok and red is poor. Yoast SEO gives you a breakdown of the areas you need to pay attention to. This acts as a checklist to ensure you have fully optimised your post.

Readability

Yoast SEO also scores your readability with the same traffic light system which shows you whether your post is optimised for readers. This tells you exactly where you can make improvements to your post to make it as reader-friendly as possible. In other words, how easy is it for them to follow? The easier it is to follow, the more engaged they are likely to be.

Preview and edit meta data

Yoast SEO also allows you to view and edit your URL, title and meta description before you post goes live. It shows you where your keyword is appearing in the titles and meta description so you can improve the optimisation.

Customise social media snippets

As well as customising your snippets for search engines, you can also customise the snippets that appear when someone shares your blog post on Facebook or Twitter.

Auto-generated XML sitemap

Yoast offers the feature of an automatically generated XML sitemap. An XML sitemap makes it easier for search engines to crawl your page. Refer to the chapter 'X is for XML Sitemap' for further information on this.

SEO management

Yoast SEO has a lot of features that take care of the more technical SEO aspects of your site. There is a lot of background stuff that Yoast can do for you, so you don't have to worry about it.

Do you need Yoast SEO?

It isn't essential to have Yoast SEO but if you do have a WordPress site then it makes sense. After all, you want your post to get found by search engines so why wouldn't you get help with SEO? There are other SEO plugins available but Yoast is the most highly rated.

If your website isn't built in WordPress, then you should speak to your web designer about compatible plugins or SEO management for your blog.

> ### Bonus Tip
>
> *It's important that your blog is optimised for search engines, but your content should be engaging too. If you can't get your keyword in all the places suggested by Yoast then don't worry. Don't try and squeeze it in where it doesn't naturally fit just to score green. You won't get green for every point on the checklist, just aim to get green overall. The main thing to remember is that you should always write for your readers first.*

Y is for Yoast: chapter takeaways

➡ Yoast SEO is a WordPress plugin that helps you optimise your blog post

➡ When you choose your keyword, Yoast will score you on a traffic light system so you can see how optimised your post is

➡ Yoast also gives your post a 'readability' score so you know if it is easy for readers to follow

➡ You can use Yoast as an SEO checklist before you publish your post

➡ Yoast is not the only SEO plugin and if your site is not built in WordPress then you should ask your web designer about alternative SEO plugins

Related chapters

K is for Keywords

I is for Images

O is for Optimisation

X is for XML Sitemap

Zzzz

Don't send your readers to sleep with boring content

Z is for Zzzz

Don't send your readers to sleep with boring content

The last thing you want to do is send your readers to sleep with dull, boring and uninteresting content. Create blog posts that engage readers by making your posts useful, entertaining or interesting.

Always remember that your blog represents your company. Do you want to be known as boring? Do you want readers to think you haven't put any effort into your blog? Are you happy with just posting out any old rubbish?

If you want blog posts that engage readers, then you need to put a bit of effort in. Choose the right subjects, do your research, write well, edit effectively and proofread before publishing.

How to create blog posts that engage readers

Understand your target audience
Whenever you create any sales, marketing or advertising materials, the first thing you need to do is identify your target audience. If you don't know who you are trying to reach, how do you know what will interest them, where to find them or how to engage them? Think about who you are writing your blog post for before even starting to write.

Choose relevant subjects
Once you know who you are writing for it makes it easier to choose subjects. What is your target audience interested in? What problems do they need solving?

How can you help them?

Think about how much knowledge they will already have. Are you targeting beginners or are you writing to people who already have a good knowledge of your industry? For example, an employment law firm may write blog posts for small businesses who want some basic legal advice, or they could be targeting HR directors in larger companies. The way they approach a subject, the language they use, and the amount of detail would be very different for each audience.

Create unique content
Don't just rewrite the exact same posts that have been written a hundred times before. That doesn't mean don't cover the same subjects, it just means do it in a different way. Add extra detail, put a different spin on it or add some of your own personality. Refer to the chapter 'U is for Uniqueness' earlier in this book for more advice on this.

Don't use boring, repetitive language
Even if the subject is boring, the way you write about it doesn't have to be. Don't just waffle on and on; put some passion behind your blog. Add examples, stories, statistics, testimonials or case studies to make your copy more interesting and relevant.

Simply saying "you should do this" without explaining why or giving examples of where it has worked, won't make your blog post very useful to the reader.

Mix up your adjectives; don't say something is wonderful and then in the next line say something else is wonderful and then two lines later identify something else as wonderful. The adjective will lose its impact.

Minimise industry jargon and clichés. Use interesting analogies to explain complex subjects.

Choose the right format
The format of your blog can help you present your information in an interesting way. If there is a new development in your industry you can approach it in different ways. You could write it as a news story, do an interview with an expert on the subject, collate opinions from those affected or do a prediction on what it will mean for your clients.

Take time planning the layout
Don't just write a load of copy and stick it on a page. Think about the layout of your blog post. What sub-headings will you include? Are you going to use images, graphics or video? How will you link your post to other posts or pages on your site?

How your blog post is presented can attract the reader or put them off before they even read a word.

Be interested

It helps if you are interested in the subject you are writing about as this will come across in your blog post. Think about why you are writing your blog. Do you want to help your clients? Have you got useful information to share? Do you want to entertain people? If you have a purpose behind your post it makes it more enjoyable to write.

Z is for Zzzz: chapter takeaways

➡ Your blog represents your company, so be interesting

➡ Understand your target audience and choose interesting subjects

➡ Think about the format and layout

➡ Don't use boring, repetitive language

➡ Be interested in the subject yourself and your passion will show in your writing

Related chapters

F is for Format

L is for Layout

U is for Uniqueness

W is for Writing

Glossary

Acronym: an abbreviation formed of the first letter of other words; for example, SEO=search engine optimisation

Adjective: a word that describes something

Alt tag: a description inserted into a web page to help search engines and website visitors understand the nature of the content of an image.

Anchor text: clickable text within an online document that links to another page or website.

Clickbait: headline or content designed to get readers to click through to a specific web page, often by exploiting curiosity.

Click-through-rate: the rate of visitors who click on a link that directs them through to a web page.

Copy: the text part of a blog or any other sales, advertising or marketing works

Hyperlink: a link from one webpage to another part of the web or an external document.

SEO: search engine optimisation (refer to the chapter 'O is for Optimisation').

Serif/sans-serif: a serif is a small line added to the end of the strokes of a letter, commonly used in typewriter style fonts. Popular serif fonts include Times New Roman and Courier. Sans-serif are typefaces without serifs such as Ariel.

Infographic: a visual representation of information such as a chart, pictograph or diagram.

Screen- reader: an assistive piece of software that reads text out loud from a screen to aid blind or visually impaired readers.

RSS: a web feed that allows internet users to receive content updates such as news, weather and blogs in a standardised format.

URL: Uniform Resource Locator; the URL is a web page address.

WordPress: a publishing software and content management system that offers free or paid options. Used for creating websites and blogs.

XML sitemap: refer to the chapter 'X is for XML sitemap'.

Yoast: refer to the chapter 'Y is for Yoast'.

Appendix 1: Weasel words

Very	Great	Obviously
Really	Like	Occasionally
That	Nice	Basically
Quite	Help	Probably
Just	Various	Practically
Could	Every	Actually
Can	Several	Possibly
Might	Many	Virtually
May	Rather	Totally
Good	About	Usually
Often	Nearly	Slightly
Most	Fairly	Extremely
Some	Surely	Suddenly
Kind of	Sort of	Exceedingly

Appendix 2: Example blog planner

Type	Title/subject	Write date	Edit date	Post date
How-to	How to generate blog ideas	7th Jan	14th Jan	21st Jan
List	Top 10 websites for free images	14th Jan	21st Jan	28th Jan
Checklist	SEO checklists for bloggers	21st Jan	28th Jan	4th Feb
Inform	5 Benefits of starting a blog	28th Jan	4th Feb	11th Feb

Appendix 3: Generating ideas

- Ask customers/suppliers/social media followers

- Research competitor blogs and blogging sites

- Go on forums and see what questions people ask

- Current trends

- Seasonal posts

- News

- 'The story so far'- company history

- Frequently asked questions

- Biggest myths or misconceptions surrounding your industry/sector/company

- Do a survey and write a post around the results

- Write up a talk or presentation you did

- Industry advice for beginners

- Top tips

- Checklists

Appendix 4: Power words

Free	Unbeatable	Hazardous
Extra	Revolting	Stupid
Bargain	Illegal	Volatile
Best	Backlash	Warning
Discount	Beware	Victim
Instant	Caution	Deadly
Bonus	Rare	Arrogant
Prize	Danger	Lying
Profit	Deadly	Hate
Now	Devastating	Scary
Only	Disastrous	Crisis
Reduced	Targeted	Danger
Sale	Toxic	Shocking
Rich	Mistake	Basic
Save	Revenge	Simple
Prestigious	Crucial	Easy
Secret	Critical	Effortless
Exclusive	Vital	Painless
Preview	Paramount	Suffer
Limited	Hopeless	Exposed
Special offer	Sabotage	Increase
Controversial	Alarming	Immediately
Agonising	Disturbing	Heart-breaking
Elite	Excruciating	Struggle
Useful	Emergency	Hoax

A note from the author

Thank you for purchasing the 'A-Z of Blogging'. I hope you've enjoyed reading it as much as I enjoyed writing it. Most of all, I hope that you've found the contents useful.

This book originally started out as a series of blogs, before it was suggested by a client that I turn it into a book. As soon as she said it I realised how much sense it made.

What I love about blogging is that anyone can share their ideas, thoughts or knowledge with the world. You don't even need a fancy website; just the motivation to write and the confidence to share.

I hope I have inspired you to communicate your stories and ideas through the written word too.

I'd like to say a huge thank you to everyone who has helped make this book possible. In particular; my mum who taught me to read, write and follow my dreams, and my husband who has supported me every step of the way. A special mention to Tina, whose idea it was to write this book and to Rick who agreed to help me get it out to the world. Thanks for all your support and advice.

Lisa